ONE IS NOT A PAIR

a spotting book

Britta Teckentrup

It's sunny and warm,
and the sky is so blue,
just right for some ice cream.
I'd like one—would you?

Take a close look;
there's a match for each cone.
Can you find the one
that is all on its own?

Black-and-white magpies
are building their nests.
They strut and they prance
and they puff out their chests.

Each bird has found something
that its mate also holds.
But one magpie's treasure
is made out of gold.

Here's a squadron of planes,
so fearless and proud.
It's perfect for flying
amid all the clouds.

As they circle the globe,
each plane has a pair.
But one does not match
as it zooms through the air.

Here is a farmyard
where tractors are puffing,
wheels are a-spinning,
and engines are huffing.

There's two of each tractor—
but there's an exception.
You'll see one is different
if you use your perception.

These shiny red cherries
look tasty and sweet,
and some hungry young bees
have stopped for a treat.

The bees are all happily
feasting on lunch,
but which group of fruits
matches no other bunch?

These red-and-white toadstools
are covered in spots,
and the ladybugs, too,
have splendid black dots.

Match up the toadstools—
there are two of each kind.
But there's one with no mate,
which you have to find!

Chirping and cheeping,
birds hop all about
their new wooden houses,
both inside and out.

Each birdhouse and bird
is matched, two by two,
except for one songbird.
I see her; can you?

The birds have now flown
to the tops of the trees,
where they tweet and they twitter
and sing in the breeze.

Each tree has a mate
where matching birds call.
But one has a guest
that is no bird at all.

On a shelf in the store
are cuddly brown bears,
and each bear has a friend,
for these bears come in pairs.

There are two of each teddy,
but one's all alone.
Perhaps he's the one
who most needs a new home.

With bright wooden blocks
you can spend hours and hours,
making cool houses
and building tall towers.

Each one has a match
identically laid.
Can you see the one that
is differently made?

They prowl and they preen,
they mew and they purr,
these yowling black cats
with sleek, shiny fur.

One cat's not the same
though he's slinky and thin.
Can you find the cat
that is missing a twin?

When autumn arrives,
leaves fall to the ground,
where insects are creeping
and crawling around.

Each leaf and each beetle
is matched by another.
But one of these creatures
is missing his brother.

A new box of pencils
in colors so bright
are all newly sharpened
and ready to write.

There's two of each color,
some red and some green,
but one does not match—
is it one that you've seen?

Stripy and spotty
and pinned up in rows,
socks dance on a line
as the wind briskly blows.

It's hard not to find
each matching sock pair,
but one has no mate—
can you see it up there?

And now here are pairs
of all that you've seen;
pairs of pencils and planes
and of cats, black and lean.

Can you spot each pair?
And when you are done,
can you find the thing
of which there's just one?

First U.S. edition 2017

Library of Congress Catalog Card Number pending
ISBN 978-0-7636-9319-0

16 17 18 19 20 21 TLF 10 9 8 7 6 5 4 3 2 1

Printed in Dongguan, Guangdong, China

This book was typeset in Brown.
The illustrations were created digitally.

BIG PICTURE PRESS
an imprint of
Candlewick Press
99 Dover Street
Somerville, Massachusetts 02144

www.candlewick.com